THE ENERGY BROTHERS

Hydrogen

Helium

Benedict Maresca

ISBN 978-1-957220-42-0 (paperback)
ISBN 978-1-957220-43-7 (digital)

Copyright © 2022 by Benedict Maresca

All rights reserved. No part of this publication may be reproduced, distributed, or transmitted in any form or by any means, including photocopying, recording, or other electronic or mechanical methods without the prior written permission of the publisher. For permission requests, solicit the publisher via the address below.

Rushmore Press LLC
1 800 460 9188
www.rushmorepress.com

Printed in the United States of America

THE ENERGY BROTHER

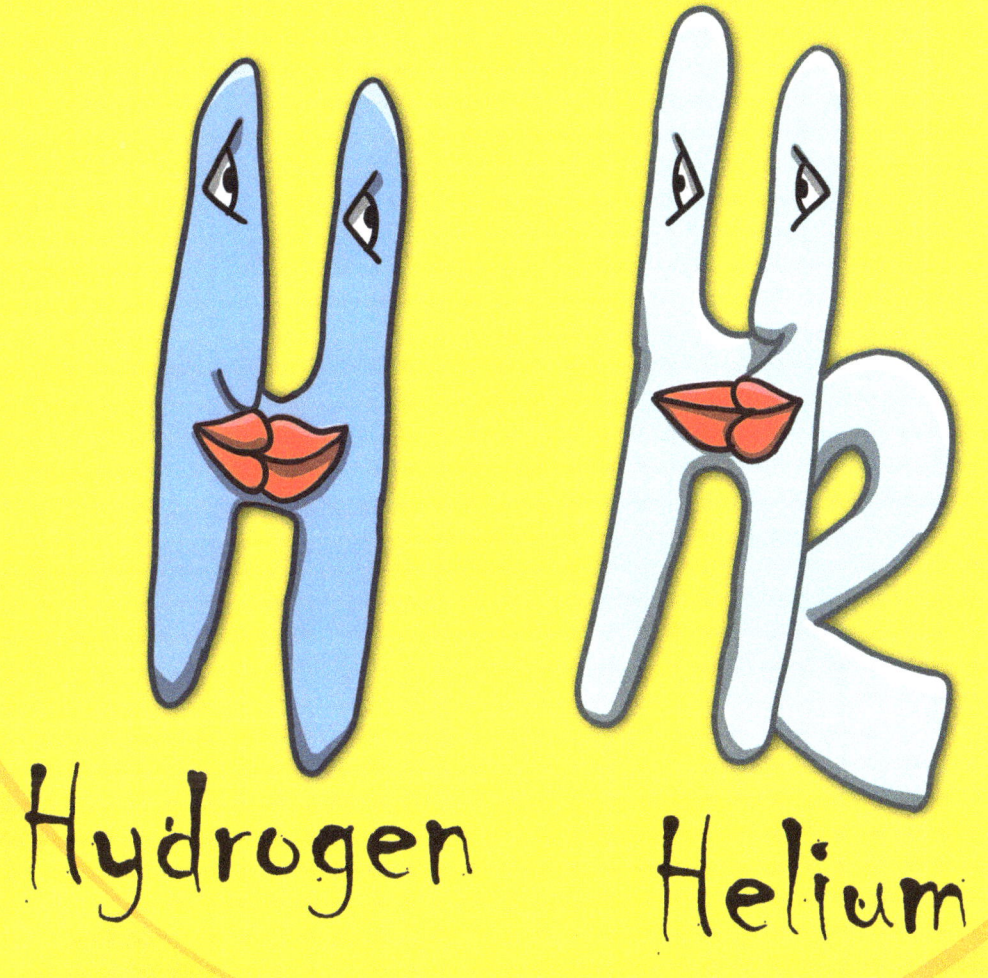

Hydrogen   Helium

I AM HYDROGEN. I AM AN ATOM, AND HAVE ONE ELECTRON AND ONE PROTON. I AM THE SMALLEST ELEMENT IN THE UNIVERSE, AND THE MOST ABUNDANT. ELEMENTS OR ATOMS ARE THE BUILDING BLOCKS OF THE UNIVERSE. THERE IS MORE OF ME THAN ANYTHING ELSE IN THE UNIVERSE.

I AM HELIUM, THE SECOND SMALLEST ATOM IN THE UNIVERSE. I HAVE 2 ELECTRONS AND 2 PROTONS.

I AM AN ATOM, WHICH IS ONE OF THE BUILDING BLOCKS OF THE UNIVERSE. THE UNIVERSE IS EVERYTHING AROUND YOU. I AM THE SECOND MOST ABUNDANT ELEMENT OR BUILDING BLOCK IN THE UNIVERSE.

HYDROGEN ATOMS LIKE TO RUN AROUND AND WHEN IT IS REAL HOT THEY SMASH INTO EACH OTHER. WHEN THIS HAPPENS WE TURN INTO HELIUM ATOMS.

WHEN WE TURN INTO HELIUM, LIKE WHAT HAPPENS IN THE SUN AND STARS, WE GIVE OFF A LOT OF ENERGY LIKE HEAT AND LIGHT. WHEN WE SQUEEZE TOGETHER AND BECOME HELIUM IT IS CALLED FUSION. ALL THE LIGHTS FROM STARS AT NIGHT ARE FROM THE ENERGY BROTHERS LIGHT.

HELIUM IS THE SECOND LIGHTEST ELEMENT AFTER HYDROGEN. IT IS SO LIGHT, WHEN YOU FILL A BALLON WITH ME, IT MAKES THE BALLON FLOAT AWAY.

HYDROGEN IS THE SMALLEST AND LIGHTEST ELEMENT IN THE UNIVERSE, AND FLOATS BALLONS LIKE HELIUM, BUT HYDROGEN IN VERY FLAMABLE, AND CAN CATCH ON FIRE AND EXPLODE. THIS HAPPENED TO A BALLON SHIP CALLED THE HINDENBURG IN 1937. IT EXPLODED AND WAS DESTROYED.

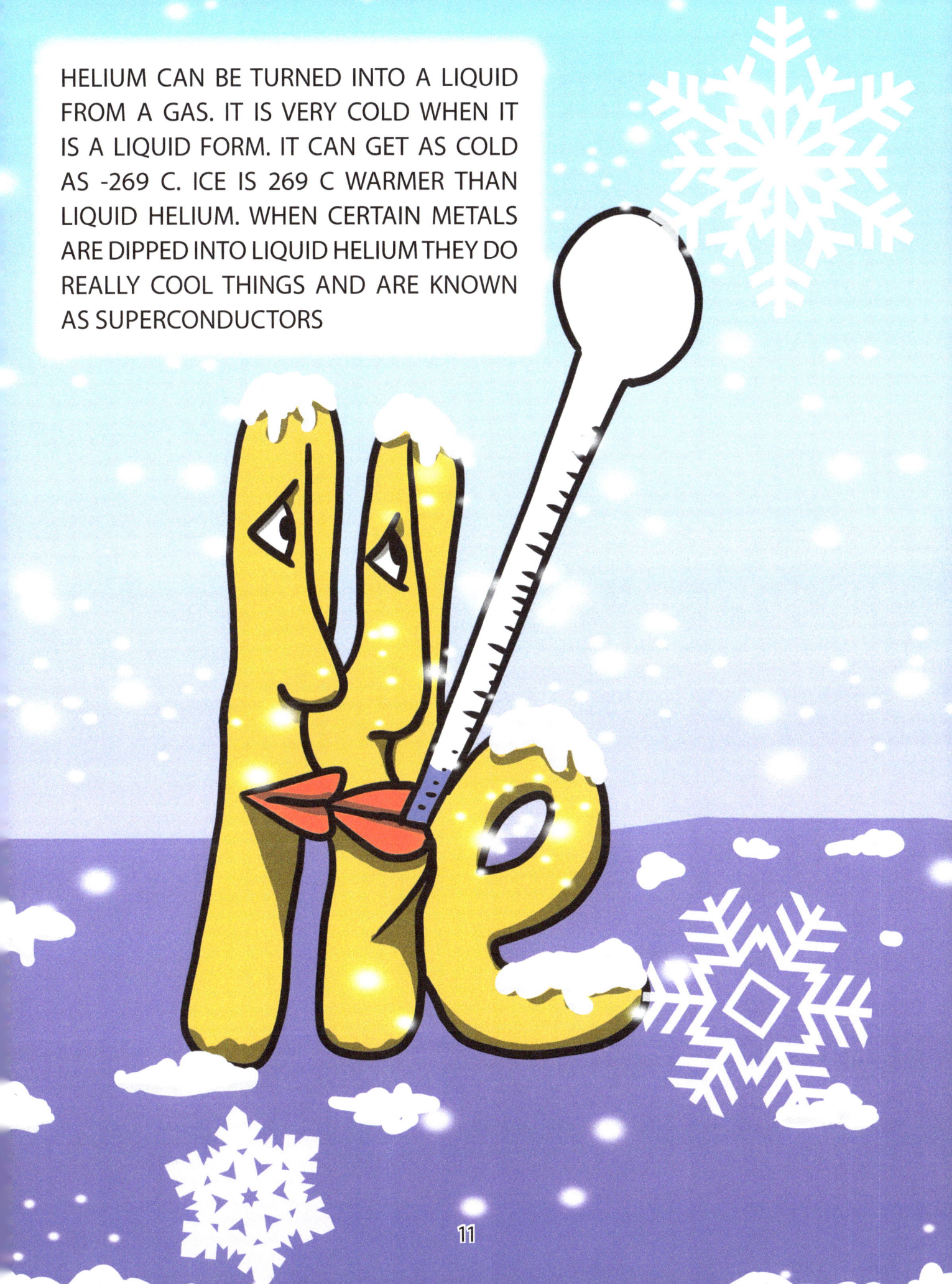

HYDROGEN IS PRESENT ALL AROUND US. IT COMBINES WITH OXYGEN (ANOTHER TYPE OF ELEMENT) TO FORM WATER. HUMANS ARE MADE OF 70% WATER AND WATER MAKES UP 71% OF THE EARTH.

WATER IS FORMED WHEN HYDROGEN IS BURNED.

HYDROGEN IS WHAT MAKES THINGS TASTE SOUR, LIKE VINEGAR, LEMONS, AND PICKLES. THE SOUR TASTE MEANS IT IS ACIDIC.

THE ENERGY BROTHERS BIG JOB IS TO KEEP THE SUN HOT AND BRIGHT. IT IS 15,000,000 C. THAT IS REALLY HOT. WATER BOILS AT 100 C. THE OTHER IMPORTANT JOB WE DO IS CREATE GRAVITY, WHICH IS A FORCE THAT KEEPS ALL 9 PLANETS IN THE SOLAR SYSTEM RUNNING AROUND THE SUN. THE PLANETS GO AROUND THE SUN IN A PATH THAT IS CALLED AN ORBIT. IF THE ENERGY BROTHERS DID NOT PLAY AROUND AND MAKE THE SUN, THE PLANETS WOULD FLOAT AWAY AND LIFE WOULD NOT EXIST ON EARTH.

ANIMALS LIKE HUMANS INHALE THE OXYGEN AND EXHALE THE CARBON DIOXIDE. THIS IS CALLED THE CARBON CYCLE. THIS IS WHY PLANTS ARE SO IMPORTANT TO OUR EXISTANCE. THIS IS WHY RAIN FORESTS AND TREES ARE SO IMPORTANT.

THE ENERGY BROTHERS ARE RESPONCIBLE FOR THE SUN BEING ABLE TO HEAT THE EARTH, AND GET THE PHOTOSYNTHESIS GOING IN PLANTS FOR THE CARBON CYCLE. IF THE ENERGY BROTHERS DID NOT DO THEIR JOB LIFE WOULD NOT EXIST.

THE ENERGY BROTHERS ALSO HELP THE SUN MAKE LIGHT AND SENDS IT TO EARTH TO MAKE ELECTRICITY FROM SOLAR PANELS.

THE ENERGY BROTHER

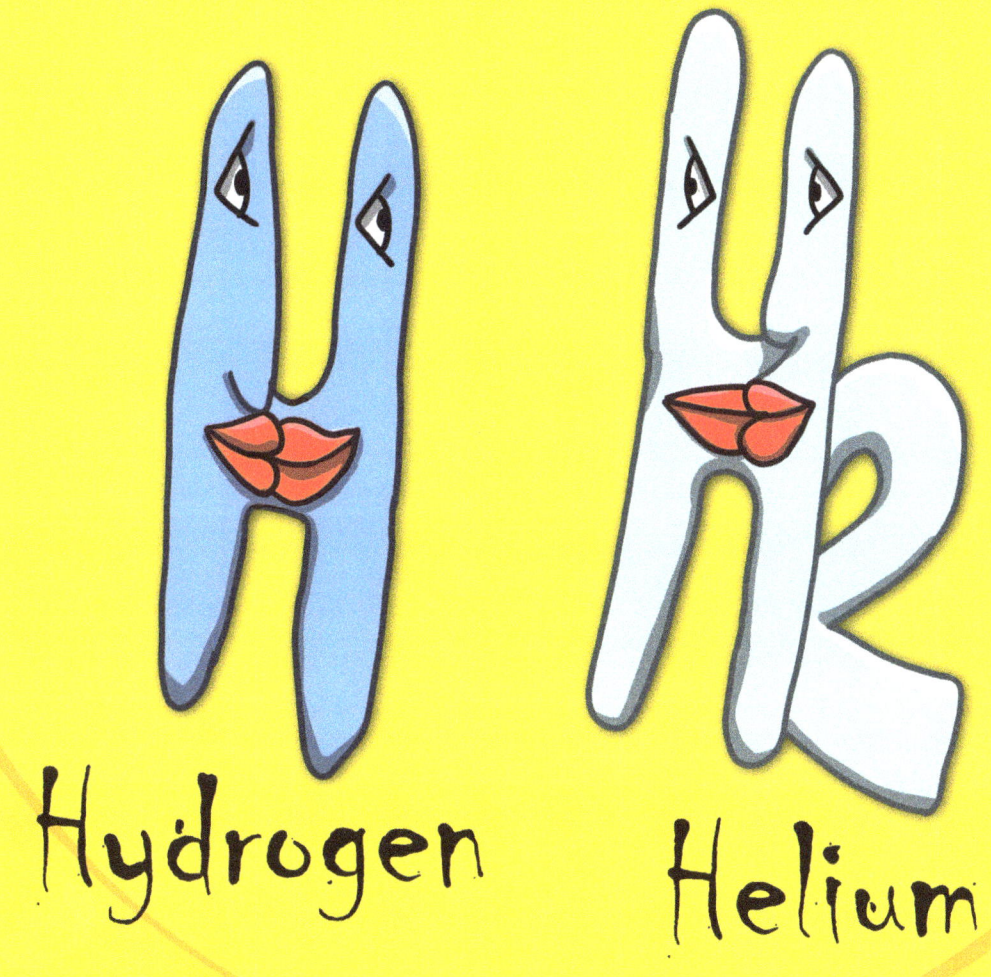

Hydrogen   Helium

SO NEXT TIME YOU LOOK AT THE STARS AT NIGHT, OR AT THE SUN, SAY THANKS ENERGY BROTHERS, OR BREATH IN CLEAN AIR OR EAT SOME FRESH VEGATABLES OR FRUITS, SAY THANKS ENERGY BROTHERS, OR FEEL THE WARMTH OF THE SUN, SAY THANKS ENERGY BROTHERS.

www.ingramcontent.com/pod-product-compliance
Lightning Source LLC
Chambersburg PA
CBHW061108070526
44579CB00011B/184